This book is for anyone who's ever felt stuck, scared to take risks, or plagued by self-doubt. You're not alone in those feelings. Trust me, I've been there too!

I hope this book serves as a beacon of hope and inspiration, guiding you to discover your true potential and reminding you that you are special and unique. Embrace your journey, believe in yourself, and never forget the power that lies within you. You've got something special to offer the world, even if you haven't quite figured out what it is yet.

May you find the courage to chase your dreams and shine brightly in this world. You've got this!

With warmth and encouragement,
Shannon

It was another Monday morning in the break room,

Just ten minutes past nine, and
Maggie was already having
an existential crisis.

She was at her five-year workiversary
party, where she was listening to her
four closest strangers make small talk.

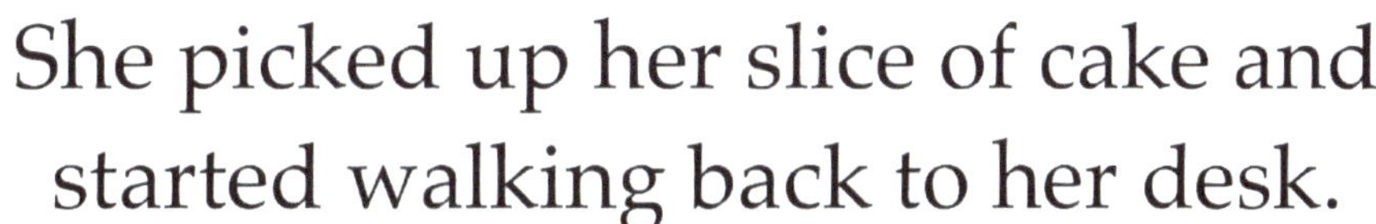

She picked up her slice of cake and
started walking back to her desk.

Maggie sat down at her desk and took a long look at her coffee mug.

Then she smiled, sat a little taller, and got to work.

Maggie took pride in her work and enjoyed it. In some ways, it was an escape she could rely on throughout her life.

YOU GOT THIS

She stared intensely at her screen while she took one hand off the keyboard to take her first bite of the workiversary cake.

Holy cottonmouth! The cake was so terribly dry she could barely choke it down.

Normally, she didn't take many breaks throughout the day, but this certainly merited a visit to the water cooler… so, she walked to the break room and poured a glass of water.

Now she could get back to work.

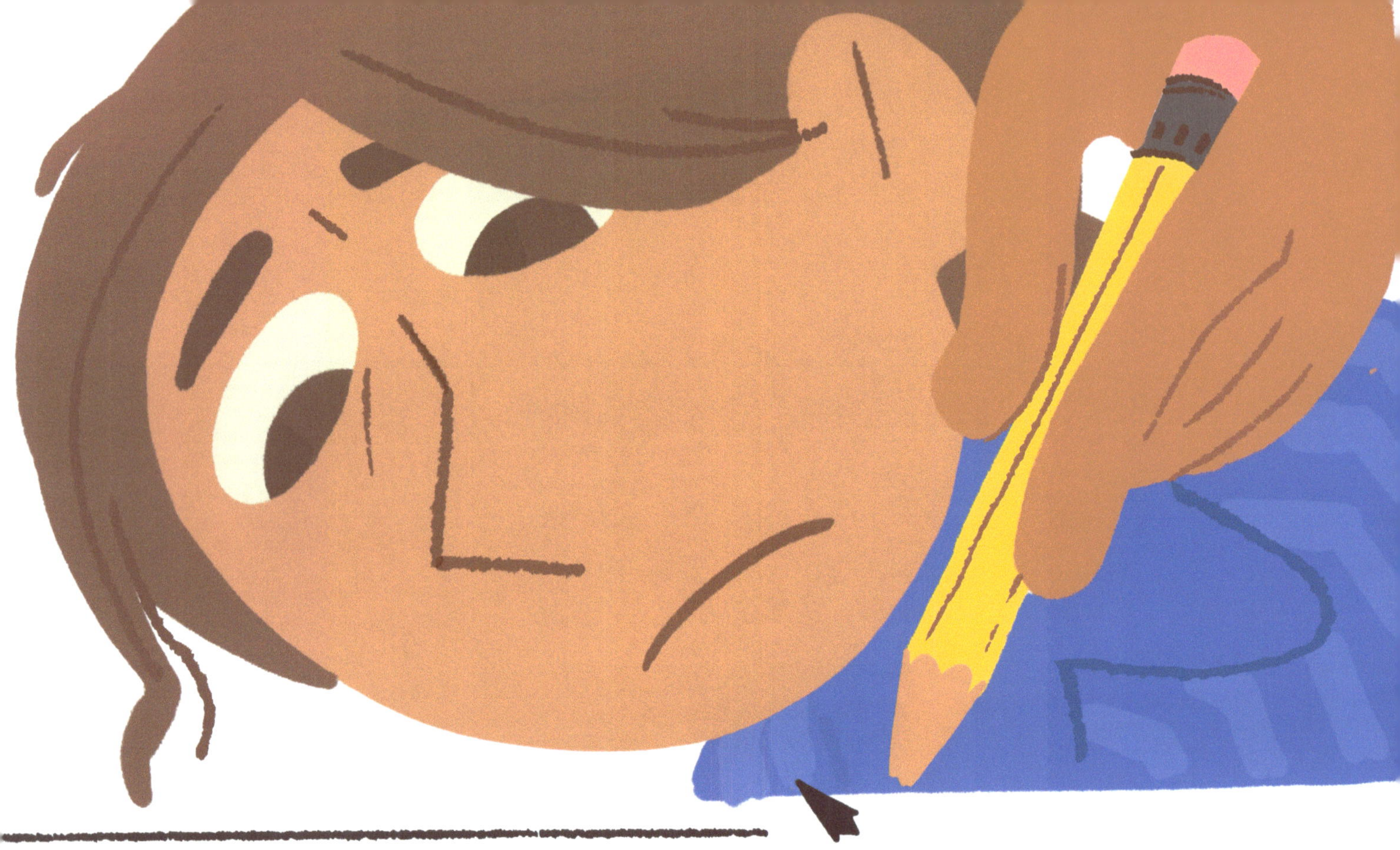

Back at her desk, she chose a colored pencil and started to sketch, when the point broke. She walked to the pencil sharpener and ground it to a fine point.

Now she could get to work.

Maggie chose another pencil only to realize that ALL the pencils were dull. So, she scooped them up, walked them to the pencil sharpener and inserted each one until it was perfectly pointed.

Now she could definitely get back to work.

But not before she felt a familiar slap on her back…. It was Todd.

by Todd
YAGGIE

Todd was always borrowing Maggie's meeting notes. Todd tricked Maggie into creating his presentations for him. Todd stole Maggie's lunch on many occasions despite it being clearly marked.

"How's it going, Maggie? Did you happen to do those monthly reports Gregg asked us for? They're due soon and you know how Gregg is!" he said, rolling his eyes.

Maggie didn't remember monthly reports being in her job description. But she was a team player, so she let Todd know she'd take care of it.

She didn't mind doing the monthly reports. It really was no trouble. She'd just have to stay a few hours late again, which was well worth the time saved on hearing another speech from Gregg and seeing that toady Todd nod along in the corner of a conference room.

EMPLOYEE
OF
THE
MONTH

EMPLOYEE
OF
THE
MONTH

EMPLOYEE
OF
THE
MONTH

Halfway into the monthly reports she heard the familiar "Beep… beep… beep!" of her phone. Five o'clock. Time to call it a day. But not for Maggie.

At around 7:30pm, she sat back in her chair, pleased. In addition to her newly sharpened pencils and surviving the near-death cake experience, she had gotten a ton of work done.

However, as she packed her things, a photo of her on the beach caught her attention.

She felt such joy and peace there, listening to the crashing waves and feeling the warm sand between her toes. She felt Inspired. Creative.

Did she feel that joy now?

She couldn't shake this feeling that was becoming harder to ignore as each work day passed… wasn't she meant for something more?

It was Tuesday morning in the break room,

where Maggie was absentmindedly watching her mug fill up with the coffee that would get her through the day.

She was half-listening to her co-workers recall how their boss, Gregg, made inappropriate jokes at a party last night as he guzzled his seventeenth beer when she heard, "Congratulations on your promotion, Todd!"

Todd got a promotion?

When she arrived at her desk, the words, "Todd got a promotion," were still echoing in her ears.

She watched as the cursor line blinked at her… she blinked back.

 She decided to pull up a job site. "Just to see what's out there," she thought.

She pulled up one position and discarded it… surely there are smarter people than her that could do that job…

 She pulled up the second listing, read the job description and closed it… she didn't meet every qualification listed in that one. She'd probably need more experience.

The third listing looked promising. But she couldn't do that job because she decided it would require her to start over… and starting over was far too scary and too risky.

She looked again at her photo on the beach and thought maybe she could be a surf instructor in Hawaii. Although that would require knowing how to surf and knowing how to teach someone how to surf…

No, she should stick to what she knows. She knows this job… she *kind* of knows her boss…

She decided to give Gregg a visit.

On her way to Gregg's office, she couldn't help but notice how dry the plants looked, so she gave her chlorophylled co-workers a drink (sure, they hadn't had any of the left over workiversary cake, but boy did they look thirsty) before finally arriving at Gregg's door.

She knocked…

Nothing.

Knocked again…

Still nothing. She turned the doorknob
and asked, "Gregg? Are you here?"

No Gregg.

Thinking he must've run to the bathroom, she took a seat. As she waited, she looked around at the things that were proudly displayed on his desk.

Maggie listened to the clock on the wall tick… tick… tick… when she heard - breathing?

The type of breathing that comes from a portly man with what she could only imagine was an undiagnosed deviated septum.

She followed the sound, going from the desk to the floor, when she noticed something peculiar…

"Gregg?" she asked, hesitantly. "Gregg… are you under the desk?"

A grumble came from under the desk and he emerged, all five foot two of him stood and took a look at the clock before plopping down in his chair.

"I was just looking for my uh… pen that I dropped… gum?"

Maggie took a long, deep breath and said, "Gregg, as you know, I've been with the company for five years now."

"Yeah, I'm sorry I missed your workiversary party; was it a real rager? Hehe," Gregg snorted.

"It was a riot… so anyway," Maggie continued, "I wanted to talk to you about my future here. Lately I've been feeling a lack of recognition for my work, which has me feeling a bit unmotivated."

Gregg started to rearrange things on his desk. First, he shuffled a pile of papers, then he straightened his pens.

Not making eye contact, he leaned back in his chair, scratched the protruding belly that he'd earned from his beer pong champion days, then leaned forward and said, "Sure, we can work on that! Why don't you talk to the HR department more about that. Yeah… they should be able to help!"

Maggie slowly got up from her chair, not sure how to process Gregg passing her off to HR, before finally mustering a half hearted "thank you".

 "Sure thing! I can't be a player without a team! Just remember to keep your eye on the ball!" Gregg shuffled her out of his office.

Just as Maggie settled back at her desk and booked a meeting with HR, she heard the familiar "Beep… beep… beep," notifying her it was five o'clock. Time to call it a day.

As she slid her things into her backpack, she couldn't help but wonder if this was really what she wanted to do with her life. Sure, she had gotten a ton of work done; she had taken a step forward by meeting with her boss… and let's not forget the altruistic plant watering…

But, wasn't she meant for something more?

It was Wednesday morning in the break room.

Maggie was filling up her cup, daydreaming of her toes in the sand and the ocean breeze in her hair when she heard a familiar voice…

"Hump Day. Not as depressing as Monday, not as exciting as Friday, am I right, Mag?!"

She looked up at Todd, towering over her. All six, gangly feet of him, grinning smugly.

She examined his discolored grin and thought it curious that his own teeth weren't friends with each other before exclaiming a reluctant, "Yep!" and hurriedly walked away.

She reached her desk, feeling excited, because today was the day she would speak with HR!

She imagined a conversation buzzing with ideas, two professionals brainstorming all the things Maggie could do for the company that could get her out of this funk.

She was excited to get started on a project where her work would be recognized. She was excited to start working on something that made her feel the joy she felt when she looked at that photo of her on the beach.

 She imagined for a moment what it'd be like to *work* on the beach. Maybe she could be one of those yoga instructors who walked people through yoga flows on the sand, smelling the ocean as the waves crashed on the shore.

Of course, that would require her to take up yoga, and then get her yoga certification. Would she need some sort of permit to do that? She shook the thoughts out of her head, gathered her things, and headed toward the HR office.

PASSION

TEAMWORK

INTEGRITY

KINDNESS

HANG IN
THERE

KEEP CALM
human resources
IS HERE

HR PROFFESSIONAL

She stepped into the HR office and took a seat. "Hey Cindy!" Maggie started. "Gregg suggested I speak with you about how I've been feeling lately about my job." Maggie explained how her work felt unrecognized, and she wanted to discuss a way forward.

Once Maggie had finished talking, Cindy inserted one long, acrylic fingernail into her hair pouf and scratched. Her hair never moved, but when she was finished, she'd left her enormous diamond ring behind.

"Maggie? If you were a type of cookie," Cindy paused to emphasize the seriousness of the question, "what type would you be?"

"Err… snickerdoodle?" Maggie answered.

"Noooo Maggie," Cindy said, shaking her head. "The answer is chocolate chip. A chocolate chip cookie is loyal and something people can rely on. So!" she said emphatically, "I want you to think on that."

Speechless, Maggie mustered a half-hearted head nod, stood up, and left the office.

She headed to the break room for a glass of water.
Had she stepped into an alternate dimension?

As she walked, feeling nothing like a chocolate chip
cookie, she had a vision.

She saw herself in this very office with the flickering fluorescent lights and beige walls. Her hands were wrinkled and her hair had grayed. She was working on a monthly report when, in the vision, she looked at that photo.

That photo of herself, young and happy on the beach.

When she got to her desk, she found a note that said, "Thanks for stopping by! -Cindy" and under the note was a cookie.

Chocolate chip.

She decided to pull up a few more job listings.

Why couldn't she start over? What was so scary about that? Suddenly, for a brief moment, starting over didn't seem as scary as imagining herself well into her retirement years still doing Todd's reports.

A job listing grabbed her attention. It read,
"You can work anywhere!"

"Anywhere?!" she thought. As she stared
at the screen, she found herself on the
beach again. But this time, with a
computer in hand.

She could almost feel the warmth of the sand between her toes when the ping of a new email brought her back to her cubicle.

She stared at the email blankly and her mind started to race. Could she stay here? Should she stay here? If she were to leave, wouldn't all her hard work go down the drain? All the hours she'd put into this company. Would that all be for nothing?

"Beep… beep… beep," sang the familiar
sound of her phone. Five o'clock again.

She was still staring at that email from
Todd when the familiar thought crossed
her mind…

Wasn't she meant for something more?

It was Thursday morning in the break room

and Maggie was lost in thought as her mug filled up with the familiar smell of the cheap break room coffee.

She was thinking she should give this place another chance. She didn't want all her hard work to go down the drain, and she didn't love the idea of starting over. It was scary.

So, Maggie decided to do something bold. Today, she was going to talk to the C.E.O.

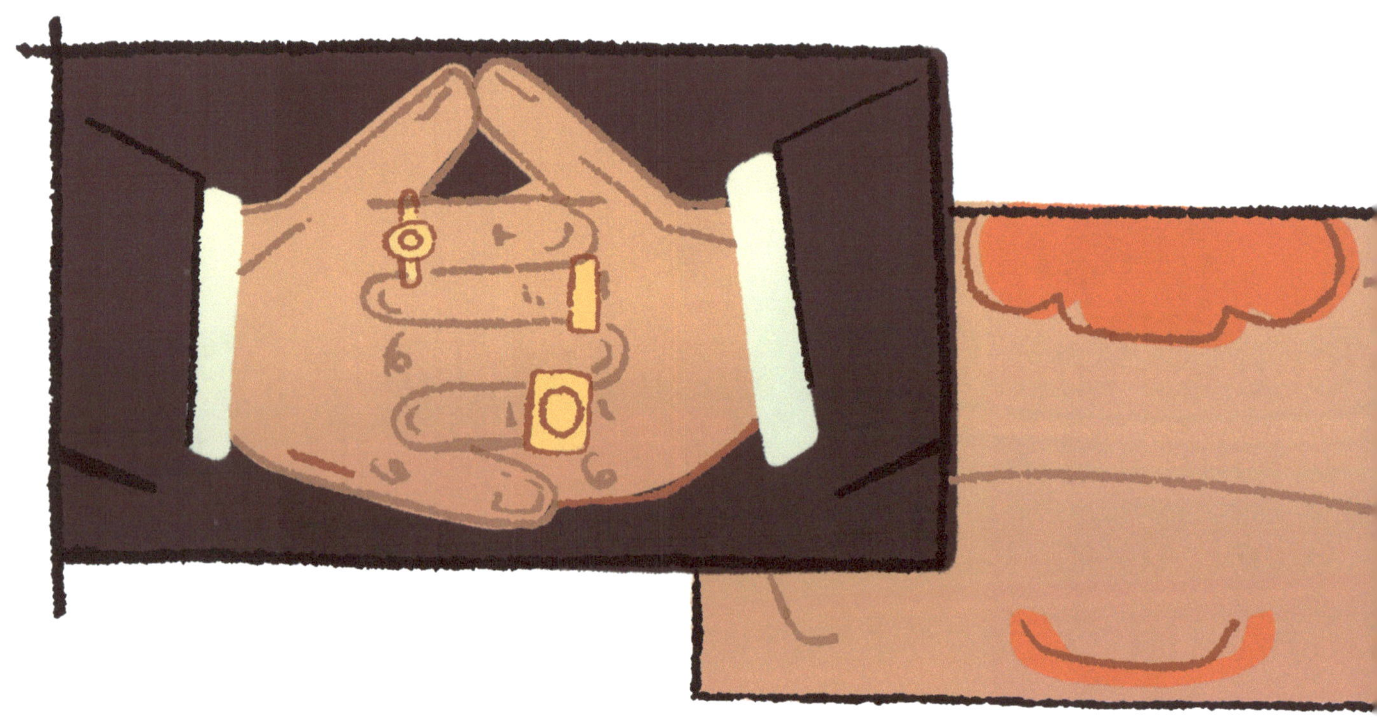

He was known to be a real tyrant and
terribly impatient. No one had ever seen
him before, not even Gregg.

And it was rumored that he was not one for
interruptions.

Maggie took a moment to read the words on her coffee mug before walking to her desk.

She looked at her to-do list, and was relieved to escape into work for a few hours before memorizing what she'd say to the CEO.

At 1 p.m Maggie finished up her work and started the long walk to the CEO's office. Surely, he couldn't be that scary. Surely, he'd understand where she was coming from.

After all, she was trying to stay. She just needed a little bit of clarity. A little bit of recognition for all her hard work.

She walked for what seemed like an eternity. With every step, the walls seemed to become more and more colorless. The carpet smelled like that of a musty motel in need of a renovation. Was the hallway getting narrower?

 She finally arrived at the CEO's office and looked up at the arched, ornate wooden door. She took notice of the matching vertical handles as the door loomed in front of her.

She lifted her fist in the air, took a deep breath, and then knocked three times.

Behind the door, she heard a grumble and then an impatient, "COME IN!"

Maggie pulled one of the big handles with both hands, her heart beating loudly in her chest, and walked in.

She cleared her throat. "Hi Mr. Maloney. I'd like to talk to you about my role here and discuss with you what I've accomplished so far along with what I'd like to contribute to the company moving forward".

Max Maloney's chair slowly turned.

She was surprised by his small stature. She wondered for a moment why those few scraps of hair still clung to the rim of his head. Determination, she thought.

He leaned forward, perched his elbows on the desk, raised his eyebrows and impatiently said, "Well, TAKE A SEAT."

She started off by letting Max know all the accomplishments she was proud of during her five years with the company.

She talked about how she'd managed 500-plus customer accounts while maintaining a 100% customer satisfaction rating. She told him how she implemented an efficient sales funnel, directly increasing sales by 30%.

She talked about how she'd cut company spending and reduced software costs by proposing new strategies. She'd created the company's training manual and had trained most of the staff that is currently on the team.

 She could hear the excitement in her voice as she recalled all of her accomplishments.

She let him know that though she is proud of all the work she's done so far, she's looking for more recognition. More purpose.

She explained that she had spoken with her boss and with HR, but she was still unsure of how to move forward.

What else could she do to be recognized? Were there any other projects or initiatives she could lead that could help her receive the recognition she was looking for?

"I want more…
I want more responsibility…

more recognition…
a seat at the table." She continued.

When she finished, she felt relieved.

And she waited with anticipation for his
response.

Max took his feet off the table, leaned in again, his elbows perched on the desk in his power pose and said,

"I'm sorry darlin' but... who are you again?"

Maggie felt as though the breath was knocked out of her.

She felt tears welling up from frustration, so she quickly stood up and without a word, turned on her heel and left.

She pressed her back against the door for a moment, took a deep breath, and headed back to her desk.

Her mind was racing more than ever.

She pulled up that job listing again, took a long look at how happy she was on the beach that day in the photo, and submitted her application.

She started to imagine a life where she could work and feel the ocean air on her face. She started to imagine working for a company that appreciated her. She imagined working with people who inspired her, who worked just as hard as she did.

The glare of the flickering overhead light
and the "Beep… beep… beep," of her alarm
brought her back to reality.

It was this day that she realized…

…she was meant for
something more.

It was Friday morning in the break room.

But this was no ordinary Friday.
This Friday was different.

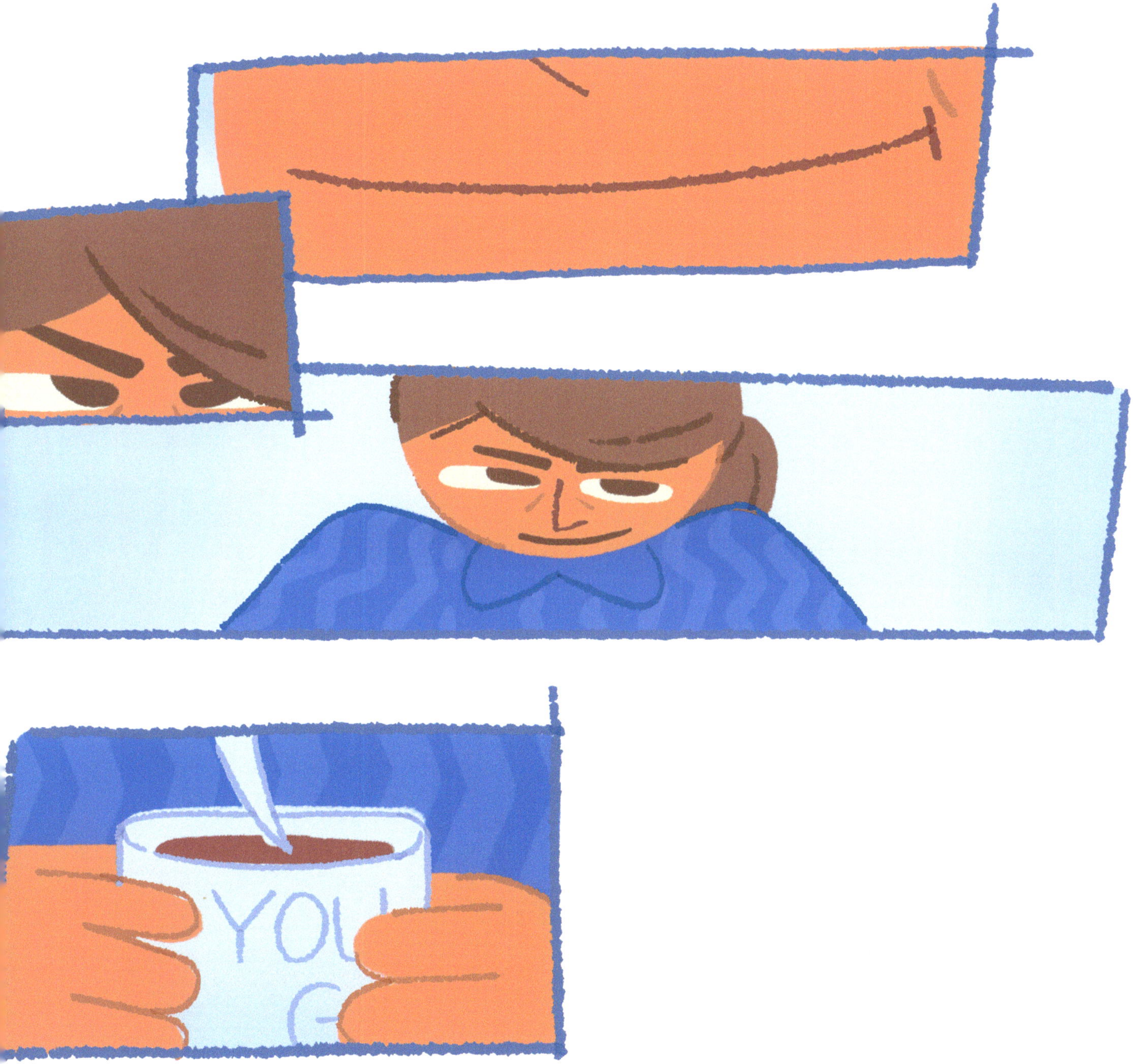

YOU

Maggie's mind swirled with the events from the week.

At her desk, she looked at the presentation showing all her accomplishments that she'd prepared for Max. And she smiled.

She worked hard and did really good work, and she took pride in that. In fact, she was starting to realize she could do this same quality of work for another company.

Why *couldn't* she start over? What was so scary about starting a new job with new people and a new boss?

Her thoughts continued to race, "What if she found a new boss who was… better? Who didn't hide? What if Maggie were excited about her job? What if… dare she think it?.. this new group of people recognized and appreciated her work?"

Maggie turned to her computer and started to type. It was hard to get started, but then the words started to flow…

She put the finishing touches on what she'd been working on, and pressed SEND.

Maggie walked to the break room, opened the refrigerator door and grabbed a clearly marked tuna sandwich.

As she savored Todd's tuna on rye, she heard the pings as each person received her email. She heard gasps and whispers. She saw heads popping up and down from cubicles like a game of Whac-A-Mole.

Todd burst into the break room and exclaimed, "Maggie! You can't leave! Where will you even go?!"

Maggie calmly wiped the
corners of her mouth and said,

"Somewhere with sand."

Hi there! I'm Shannon, a writer with a love for storytelling, yoga and comedy! I've always believed in following one's true potential, which inspired me to create "How to be a Quitter". When I'm not navigating the corporate world, you can find me traveling or curled up with a good book.

My journey is all about inspiring others to chase their dreams, bringing creativity to everyday life and fostering a community of like-minded dreamers. I'm thrilled to share my story with you and hope to inspire you along the way!

Aidan Ventimiglia is a painter and illustrator from Atlanta, Georgia. His work has been featured in everything from galleries to films to this very book! If he's not looking down at a drawing pad you can usually find him gazing up at birds.

You can find more of his work at aidanventi.com